NEW YORK CHANGING

DOUGLAS LEVERE

NEW YORK

CHANGING

REVISITING BERENICE ABBOTT'S NEW YORK

TEXT BY BONNIE YOCHELSON

PRINCETON ARCHITECTURAL PRESS   MUSEUM OF THE CITY OF NEW YORK

Published by
Princeton Architectural Press
37 East Seventh Street
New York, New York 10003

For a free catalog of books, call 1.800.722.6657. Visit our web site at www.papress.com.
Information on Douglas Levere's prints and a traveling exhibition is available at www.newyorkchanging.com.

Publication of this book has been supported by a grant from the Graham Foundation for Advanced
Studies in the Fine Arts. This book was developed in association with the Center for American Places,
Santa Fe, New Mexico and Staunton, Virginia (www.americanplaces.org).

Photo credits:
All images by Douglas Levere © 2004 Douglas Levere. All images by Berenice Abbott are the property
of the Museum of the City of New York unless otherwise noted.
page 13 (left): Castle Rock (near view), Green River, Wyo. Timothy O'Sullivan, 1872. Green River Buttes,
Green River, Wyo. (United States Geological Survey); page 13 (middle): Mark Klett and Gordon Bushaw
for the Rephotographic Survey Project, 1979. Castle Rock, Green River, Wyo.; page 13 (right): Mark
Klett, Kyle Bajakian, Byron Wolfe, and Toshi Wueshina for the Third View Project, 1997. Castle Rock,
Green River, Wyo.; page 14 (far left): Cave-of-the-Winds, Niagara Falls, American Side, etching, 1887,
from Niagara River and Falls—Lake Erie to Lake Ontario, 1886–1888 © Castellani Art Museum of
Niagara University Collection. Gift of Bethlehem Steel Corporation, 1982; page 14 (left): "American
Falls with Snow and Ice Mounds" from Arcadia Revisited © 1985 John Pfahl; page 14 (middle to far
right): Chino & Chinito 1972, 1984, 1992 © Milton Rogovin; page 18 (right): © Edie Winograde and
Lynn Shelton

Editing: Nicola Bednarek
Design: Jan Haux
Maps: Jane Sheinman

Special thanks to: Nettie Aljian, Janet Behning, Megan Carey, Penny (Yuen Pik) Chu,
Russell Fernandez, Clare Jacobson, John King, Mark Lamster, Nancy Eklund Later, Linda Lee,
Katharine Myers, Scott Tennent, Jennifer Thompson, Joseph Weston, and Deb Wood of
Princeton Architectural Press —Kevin C. Lippert, publisher

Library of Congress Cataloging-in-Publication Data
Levere, Douglas, 1966–
  New York changing : revisiting Berenice Abbott's New York / Douglas Levere ; text by Bonnie
Yochelson.
     p. cm.
ISBN 1-56898-473-1 (alk. paper)
1. Photography—New York (State)—New York—History—20th century. 2. New York (N.Y.)—Pictorial
works. 3. Abbott, Berenice, 1898– 4. Levere, Douglas, 1966– I. Yochelson, Bonnie. II. Abbott,
Berenice, 1898– Changing New York. III. Title.

TR25.N7L48 2004
779'.99747'1—dc22
                                                                                    2004005608

CONTENTS

ACKNOWLEDGMENTS

This publication would not have been possible without the help of many people. Foremost appreciation to Berenice Abbott, without whom none of this work would have been created. Thanks to photographer and educator Ellen Carey, who both challenged and mentored; Bonnie Yochelson, whose support and encouragement propelled this project; Todd Watts, photographer and printer for Abbott, who immediately saw my point and started me off with Abbot's camera.

At the Museum of the City of New York, many people contributed invaluable aid and assistance, especially director Sarah Henry, Eileen K. Morales, Marguerite Lavin, Bob Shamis, Victor Petryakov, and, formerly with the museum, Jan Seidler Ramirez, Rob Delbanyo, and Peter Simmons.

I am grateful for the work of Mark Klett, John Pfahl, and Milton Rogovin, a few of many photographers who have ignited the spark to attempt more than the transient. I would like to thank Paul Goldberger, who understood and believed in this work at first glance; Nancy Weber, Chris Hodenfield, and Buck Wolf for their way with words; George Thompson and Randy Jones at the Center for American Places, for their assistance in finding the publisher; Thomas Roma for his wholehearted support of the work in his peer review; photo editor Debbie Bondilic for asking the question "are you working on any personal projects?"; and David Friend at *Life* for initiating the first publication of this work.

Thanks to the staff at Princeton Architectural Press, who were steadfast in seeing this book through to publication, particularly editors Nicola Bednarek and Clare Jacobson and designer Jan Haux. My gratitude to the Graham Foundation for their publication grant and inclusion in their lecture series, special thanks to Roberta Feldman and Stephanie Whitlock. Thanks to Rosanne Kang for designing the book dummy.

I am grateful to everyone at the Anderson Gallery in Buffalo, New York for being the first to exhibit this work; Jurgen Nefzger, who pushed the exhibit beyond the academic; dealer Jayne Baum for her knowledge and continued support; Bob Klass, photographic printer for his expertise and advice; Jaime Wolf for assistance with the book contract; Julia Van Haaftan for her continued support; Sarah Hasted at Ricco/Maresca Gallery for insisting I title this work anew; and Jason Duval and Dorota Kolodziejczyk for brainstorming to rename this project.

My deep gratitude to New Yorkers who let me into their homes and offices to follow my determination of standing in Abbott's footsteps, including Jean-Claude Sergile, Roy Salsimun, Sid Dinsay, Janet Romanand, Eric Wachtel, Michael Brown, Ralph Torre, Paul Leyden, Selena Morris, Brian Caslin, Anne Covella Alarcon, Elaine Davis, Lennard Lewis, and Tony Peterson. For their cooperation to take the time to be in photographs I thank Srcann Zehel and her dog Ruby, Kyle Hunter, Michael A. Jones, Silas Ross, and Michael Northrop.

For their knowledge, assistance, and encouragement I am grateful to Reed Anderson, David Bemis, Jacob Blickenstaff, Frank Cesario, Jena Cumbo, Kathleen Frass, Andrew Galarneau, Phyllis Galembo, Matt Kantar, Ronald Kurtz, Victoria Leacock, Amanda Means, Bruce Morrow, Ken Schles, Maggie Soladay, Sandy Sorlien, Burke Paterson, Peter Penczer, Nina Rich, Howard Schatz, Jenny Schweitzer, Todd Stumpf, Brad Trent, and Sara Wasilausky. Unending gratitude to Jan Hodenfield, for his guidance and friendship.

Special thanks to my parents Julius and Ann Levere, who bought me my first camera and recognized and encouraged every artistic inclination along the way. And of course my wife Luci, who has been there from the beginning with love and support without measure.

FOREWORD

PAUL GOLDBERGER

In 1939, when Berenice Abbott published *Changing New York*, there was at least a reasonable chance that change would be for the good, or at least would not be viewed as an act of vandalism. The city was becoming less picturesque and more built-up, to be sure, but it was also a larger and more powerful presence on the world stage, and if progress meant a loss of some of the tiny shop fronts and pushcarts and brownstones that had given the sidewalks of New York their warmth and color, it also meant the construction of many of the buildings that are today considered among the great works of the twentieth century. When Abbott photographed New York, the city was becoming less honkytonk, but it was also getting Rockefeller Center and the Chrysler Building.

Now, of course, things are different. We are less certain that progress is to the good, since we have seen too much lost for no gain. It was one thing when, in Abbott's time, the great Century Theater on Central Park West by Carriere & Hastings was replaced by the equally pleasing Century Apartments by Irwin Chanin, but it is quite another when the Savoy-Plaza Hotel on Fifth Avenue disappears to make way for the General Motors Building, or when the amiable messes of Sixth Avenue and Third Avenue give way to dreary rows of glass boxes, as happened closer to our own time. Change is inevitable—a city that does not change will die—but it is one thing if change is perceived as a part of the organic growth of a living city, and quite another if it is perceived as a sign of decline and loss.

Abbott sought to document, not to moralize, although her brilliant photographs take on a kind of moral presence as a testament to the richness of the New York we once had, and to all the nuances of the city that she experienced. It is impossible to look at her photographs and not feel a sense of loss, but her eye is so fine and so sure that she makes us feel that loss not in terms of the easy emotion of nostalgia but rather as an expression of dignity, and of the reality of the city as a living thing. When you look at Abbott's photographs you experience the period she was documenting in the early 1930s not just as an isolated moment in time, but as part of a much larger continuum, as part of an arc of city life extending both backward and forward.

Berenice Abbott's arc, however, for most people, pretty much ends in 1939, and as *Changing New York* has increasingly become part of what can only be called the canon of classic works about New York, it has tended to be defined all the more as an album that connects us to a particular era and, for all its glory, does nothing more than this. The titling of a reprint of the work some years ago as *New York in the Thirties* seemed only to confirm the tendency to think of Abbott's work not as representing the larger idea of change and evolution in the city, but as being just a glimpse of the city at a single moment.

Douglas Levere has paid the greatest homage imaginable to Abbott in this remarkable work. He has rescued her, in a sense, from the narrow pedestal to which her great images are so often confined, and reminded us that she photographed the city not only to show us how it looked in her time, but to help us understand how much it is a living, changing thing. By bringing Abbott's work forward in time and replicating her vantage points today, Levere has revealed once again her original premise, and made change seem less like a matter of simple loss and more like a part of the ongoing life of the city. Levere has paid homage to Abbott in every one of these photographs, but he has also connected her work to the city we know today, and in so doing, he has made it resonate even more deeply in time.

PREFACE

SUSAN HENSHAW JONES

PRESIDENT AND DIRECTOR, MUSEUM OF THE CITY OF NEW YORK

Among the greatest treasures of the Photographs Collection of the Museum of the City of New York is the *Changing New York* series by Berenice Abbott. Beginning in 1935, Abbott photographed over three hundred urban scenes, which were the subject of two exhibitions at the museum, in 1937 and 1998. They remain among the most consulted and admired works in the collection, deeply evocative of their period and offering a brilliant melding of art and historical documentation.

Now, more than six decades later, Douglas Levere has meticulously rephotographed many of the scenes that Abbott captured in the 1930s. From Bowling Green to the George Washington Bridge, from Williamsburg, Brooklyn, to Rosebank, Staten Island, he has scoured the city for opportunities to stand where Abbott stood and to see what she would have seen there today. To view these images side-by-side is to understand that our city has both changed and not changed over the course of nearly three-quarters of a century.

When Abbott took her photographs, New York was emerging from possibly its most intense period of transformation. Over the course of some four decades, the skyscraper had transformed the city's skyline, the "new" immigration had transformed the city's culture, and a combination of city investment and private dollars had created a new transportation infrastructure. Everywhere, modernism mixed with tradition. Yet much that marks today's city had not yet emerged. When the project began, Rockefeller Center was under construction; the Museum of Modern Art's Fifty-third Street building was in the planning stages; there was no F.D.R. Drive, no Brooklyn Battery Tunnel, no Lincoln Center, no World Trade Center. Elevated lines rumbled overhead on many avenues in Manhattan, and the seaport bustled with trade. Yet much of the New York that Abbott's camera captured endures in many of Levere's images. Indeed, sometimes it is almost unchanged, showing how New Yorkers have adapted and creatively recycled their dense built environment.

The Museum of the City of New York is devoted to the past, present, and future of New York City. One of the most important things that this project reveals is that what the city is and what we see here today are part of a spectrum of change and continuity that stretches back across decades and, perhaps reassuringly, reaches forward into the years yet to come. Over a hundred years ago, O. Henry famously said of New York, "It'll be a great place if they ever finish it." Through the work of Berenice Abbott and Douglas Levere, we come to understand that New York City will indeed never be finished—and that we are all the richer for that fact.

REVISITING BERENICE ABBOTT'S
CHANGING NEW YORK

DOUGLAS LEVERE

Berenice Abbott's *Changing New York* project captured a modern vision of Manhattan and its surrounding boroughs in the 1930s. From 1997 to 2003, I returned to the original sites with the identical 8x10 Century Universal camera that Abbott used, at the same time of day and year Abbott's photographs were taken, revealing *New York Changing* over sixty years.

Rephotography is a tricky idea—at least it was for me. Ours is a culture that prizes originality; I grew up believing that inspiration had to come from within. While it was fine to pay homage to the acknowledged giants, stalking a ghost would be the act of an obsessive. I reacted quite negatively in 1994 when my friend Ellen Carey, professor of art at Hartford College, introduced me to the idea of choosing a photographic mentor and taking his work "beyond his life and into ours."

Three years later, I began to understand what she meant. I was at an auction preview filled with images by Man Ray, Ansel Adams, Weegee, Avedon—all brilliant; but what stopped me in my tracks was Abbott's vintage contact print *Broadway near Broome Street*, photographed in 1935, from *Changing New York*. I lived on Broome Street. Here I stood, unexpectedly looking at the view outside my building, taken six decades before. I could not help but compare and contrast. And before long I was imagining what my camera would see.

Almost every building Abbott had photographed still stood, but Broome Street back then was a two-way street paved with cobblestones. The trendy shoe store I passed every day was once the Bank of Sicily Trust. The kosher dairy restaurant in the lower right-hand corner of the photograph revealed that observant Jews in black suits populated the area that was now a major retail location. I realized I had been living in the illusion of a permanent now. My ultra-happening Broome Street would look quaint and dusty six decades into the future.

As I familiarized myself with the other images in *Changing New York*, they seemed to constitute an invitation to make new images from Abbott's vantage point. I had always had a passion for American architectural history and city planning and was especially curious about how buildings age and serve different purposes throughout their lives. Rephotographing Abbott's project would bring all my interests together. In a sense I would be collaborating with Abbott on a continuing document of New York City—a heady thought. At the same time, by embracing her work, I might discover a vision uniquely my own.

As the idea for the project began to take shape, it became clear that I needed an appropriate camera. Ellen Carey suggested I speak with Todd Watts, an art photographer who printed editions of Abbott's work for many years. Todd, who generously embraced my quest and invited

left: Broadway near Broome Street, 1935 **right:** Broadway near Broome Street, 1998
opposite: Oyster Houses, South Street and Pike Slip, 1937

me to his studio, told me that Abbott herself had considered rephotographing the project in 1954, for a book to be titled *Metropolis: Old and New*. She proposed to show "contrasts and comparisons of then and now, in all the kaleidoscopic tempo and variety of the city." But finding herself without a book contract and complaining that the increase in traffic complicated her task, she eventually dropped the idea.

In his studio Todd led me to a cabinet that held three 8x10 Century Universal field cameras, folded up like a row of bricks: one yellow, one red, and one black. His friend Stefen Petrak, a carpenter and framer, used to rebuild and paint old view cameras. Before her death, Todd offered Abbott one of these cameras, and she asked for it to be painted black with salmon fittings, but she died before he could give it to her. This was the camera Todd pulled out of the cabinet for me to begin the project.

Even with this totemic object in hand, I still had some doubts about the validity of my undertaking. I remember the relief I felt when I came across Mark Klett's book *Second View, The Rephotographic Survey Project* (1984). In the late 1970s, Klett and four other photographer-geologists rephotographed the nineteenth-century photographs of the American West by William Henry Jackson and Timothy O'Sullivan. Klett's complete documentation of each site and his meticulous camera work much impressed me and served as my model. Learning how Kletts's project was esteemed by the photographic community convinced me that I could stand in someone else's footprints and be on solid ground.

In the summer of 1997, I started visiting Abbott's sites and taking preliminary shots, still unsure whether I would continue the project. When shortly thereafter *Life* magazine became interested in my project and in February 1998 published five pairs of images, I felt I had sealed my commitment. I was further encouraged by the Museum of the City of New York's support. Bonnie Yochelson, who was just finishing her book *Berenice Abbott: Changing New York* for the museum, was very enthusiastic and recommended that my work be included in the exhibition of Abbott photographs that she was organizing at that time.

Bonnie also helped me arrive at a major technical breakthrough. I was having a hard time figuring out exactly which lenses Abbott had used. Abbott's book *A Guide to Better Photography*, published just after the completion of *Changing New York* in 1941, offered clues. In a few of the images she noted her shutter speed, aperture, and occasionally the lens, most commonly a Goerz Dagor. I began to buy Dagors, but even owning three lenses, I would still return from locations frustrated, having been unable to complete the image to the exactness I required.

When I complained to Bonnie that I did not have enough lenses, she said that Abbott had made the same complaint. She remembered that the photographer had "altered her lenses some-how." I was skeptical that Abbott would have tampered with the optics of a lens, but then Bonnie recalled, "She removed something from the lens." As a historian rather than a photographer,

left: Timothy O'Sullivan, Castle Rock (near view), Green River, Wyoming, 1872 **middle:** Mark Klett and Gordon Bushaw, Castle Rock, Green River, Wyoming, 1979 **right:** Mark Klett, Kyle Bajakian, Byron Wolfe, and Toshi Ueshina, Castle Rock, Green River, Wyoming, 1997
opposite: South Street and Pike Slip, 2002

Bonnie did not know what to make of this, but I understood instantly that Abbott must have been using convertible lenses, which could be used at more than one magnification. I had the camera at hand and removed the front element of a nine-and-a-half-inch Dagor. To my pleasure the camera focused at what I later discovered to be exactly twice the magnification. I had just doubled the amount of lenses I owned, which ensured my further success in completing my work.

In 1986, while a student at the University at Buffalo, I attended a slide lecture by John Pfahl, a landscape photographer who was just completing *Arcadia Revisited,* a photographic documentation of the Niagara River based on the 1880s etchings of Amos W. Sangster. Pfahl's proposal declared:

> I will use Sangster's drawings as point of departure for my art. I will find the places where he stood and discover which aspects of the scene have changed and which have persevered. I will try to recapture his affection for the river and to understand and reinterpret his tender and expressive responses to the scene.

His words aptly paraphrase my ambition with *New York Changing*.

Sometimes we provide our own such point of departure. In the early 1970s, Milton Rogovin created a number of portraits in Buffalo's Lower West Side, one of the city's poorest neighborhoods, and returned ten years later to photograph the same people. Rogovin visited them again in the early 1990s and in 2000, creating time sequences that spanned forty years. Every time I look at his pairs, I am struck by their power. Watching these people age over forty years in a moment makes me feel as though we have shared elapsed time.

A single photograph gives the illusion that time stops. A rephotograph lifts that illusion. In this tangling of the old and the new, the different and the same, lies the truth that Berenice Abbott understood well. All is flux; change is the only permanence. I am neither mystical nor grandiose enough to think Abbott anticipated my arrival on her scene, although I do believe her work may fairly be read as an invitation to do what I have done here. I hope that our paired works constitute a fresh invitation—not only to the rephotographers of the future but to anyone interested in urban life. Every change in our built environment reflects countless decisions. The future of our city depends, in great part, on understanding how past decisions have played out.

far left: Cave-of-the-Winds, Niagara Falls, American Side, etching, 1887 **left:** John Pfahl, American Falls with Snow and Ice Mounds, 1985
middle to far right: Milton Rogovin, Chino & Chinito, 1972, 1984, and 1992

INTRODUCTION

BONNIE YOCHELSON

At a 1996 auction preview, Douglas Levere stumbled across *Broadway near Broome Street*, a photograph taken in 1935 by Berenice Abbott that depicted the block where he lived in lower Manhattan. From this chance encounter began Levere's six-year commitment to rephotographing Abbott's epic documentation of Depression-era New York.

Berenice Abbott arrived in New York in 1918, a nineteen-year-old college dropout from Ohio. She stayed three years, living among artists in Greenwich Village and supporting herself with odd jobs, before moving to Paris. Abbott found her direction in 1923 when she became a darkroom assistant to Man Ray, who had established a thriving portrait studio. In 1926 Abbott opened her own studio and soon matched Ray's success. At the same time, she met Eugène Atget, an elderly photographer who had recently captured the attention of the avant-garde community. Abbott's interest in Atget was more than casual; she considered his lifelong dedication to photographing Paris a model of artistic achievement and integrity. When Atget died suddenly in 1927, she arranged to purchase the contents of his studio and devoted herself to furthering his reputation as well as her own career.

In 1929 Abbott returned to New York in search of an American publisher for a book on Atget. She was stunned by the rapid transformations that had occurred during her eight-year absence: business was booming and whole neighborhoods had been razed to make way for skyscrapers. Inspired by Atget's example, she resolved to give up her Paris studio and return to New York to document these dramatic changes. As soon as she arrived, however, the stock market crashed, and for five years she struggled to achieve her goal, reserving one day a week to photographing New York while teaching and working freelance. In 1935 her persistence paid off when the Works Progress Administration (WPA) agreed to fund her *Changing New York* project. In 1937 a selection of Abbott's photographs was exhibited at the Museum of the City of New York, which had served as her official sponsor, and in 1939, E. P. Dutton published 97 of the photographs in a book marketed as a guide to New York for visitors to the World's Fair. In 1940 Abbott concluded the project by presenting 305 exhibition prints to the museum. Despite financial and bureaucratic obstacles, Abbott had achieved her goal: to capture New York's "extraordinary potentialities, its size, its youth...its state of flux...approached with love void of sentimentality, and not solely with criticism and irony."[1]

Typical of *Changing New York* photographs, *Broadway near Broome Street* is a contact print from an 8x10 negative made with a large view camera mounted on a tripod (page 90). Abbott could have corrected the lens's distortion, which made the parallel sides of buildings appear to converge. She preferred retaining the effect, however, and as a result the nineteenth-century cast-iron warehouses at right and left seem to collapse upon the Italianate skyscraper, which

1 Application to John Simon Guggenheim Foundation, 1931;
Abbott Archive, Commerce Graphics Ltd Inc, New York.

stands out in relief against the strong midday sun. In Levere's near-replica of 1998, the subtle differences between then and now are apparent: the Victorian lamppost gives way to a modern one, the building at the far right has been torn down, and traffic on Broome Street has become one-way. These aesthetic and historical discoveries struck a deep chord in Levere's imagination.

Levere grew up in Roslyn Heights, a Long Island suburb of New York City. In 1989 he graduated from the State University of New York at Buffalo with a degree in design studies and a strong interest in architecture and architectural history. After college, Levere moved to New York City, where he worked as a photographer's assistant while gradually building a freelance practice photographing newsmakers for national magazines. As his career began to take shape, he searched for a photographic project independent of his commercial assignments.

Since the 1930s, dozens of photographers have taken New York as their subject. Wielding small cameras, they have prowled the city, creating an inventory of visual clichés: Coney Island bathers, Times Square revelers, zombie-like subway riders, and front-stoop matriarchs. Abbott's stark facades and empty streets presented a different New York. Using a large-format camera unsuitable for spontaneous street scenes, Abbott explored the idea that architecture is a powerful expression of the human presence; she conveyed change by juxtaposing structures of different eras within a single image. Levere intuitively understood Abbott's approach and was drawn into a dialogue with each of her photographs.

When Levere and I first met in August 1997, he was preparing a photo essay of his rephotographs for *Life* magazine. I had just finished *Berenice Abbott: Changing New York, The Complete WPA Project* and was preparing an exhibition from the Museum of the City of New York's Abbott collection. Levere was not the first photographer I encountered who had attempted to rephotograph *Changing New York*, but he was the first to do it right. Amateur photographers had tried but lacked the technical expertise, and professionals had tried but lacked the resources and dedication. With tenacity and craftsmanship equalling Abbott's, Levere persevered, working in his spare time and largely at his own expense. By attaching a transparency of Abbott's image onto his camera's ground glass, Levere determined the lens Abbott had used and adjusted his camera to reproduce her composition. From the project's research files, he noted the date of each image and rephotographed the site near that day to recapture Abbott's quality of light. If the weather was uncooperative or an obstacle presented itself, he often waited a full year before trying again. Levere's photographs were astonishingly accurate in composition, focus, and lighting, and they were surprisingly personal. Like Abbott, he waited for incidents on the street or pedestrians to enliven and humanize his carefully constructed images.

Levere and I had shared the unexpected joy of walking in Abbott's footsteps. Researching each of her photographs for my book had deepened my sense of her artistic accomplishment and of the city's history. Sensing that Levere's photographs offered a version of this experience to others, I advocated for using them in the museum's Abbott exhibition. Levere produced a video for this purpose, which consisted of sixteen pairs of then-and-now sequences, with Abbott's 1930s photographs dissolving into his 1997 images.

That New Yorkers loved the video was not surprising, since the sites were familiar to them. Its appeal was like that of a walking tour, an ever-popular public program for many exhibitions. Levere's photographs, however, were of more than local interest, and curators from the four museums that borrowed the exhibition used them in their shows. The Musée Carnavalet in Paris asked Levere to make slides so that his and Abbott's images could be seen simultaneously, and the Kunstverein in Düsseldorf gave an entire room to Levere's 11x14 prints, with copy prints of Abbott's photographs placed below them. Levere's exquisite work offered audiences the chance to contemplate Abbott's central theme of New York's perpetual change.

Levere has now rephotographed 114 of Abbott's 305 images, 81 of which appear in this book, and considers his work complete. Carrying sixty pounds of bulky photographic equipment through crowded streets, onto piers and rooftops, and over bridges was difficult enough for Abbott. Repeating the exercise sixty years later while confined to Abbott's choices proved to be even more challenging. In 1954 Abbott herself had attempted to rephotograph the sites but soon abandoned the project, complaining of increased traffic. A look at Levere's successes and failures illuminates how city life has changed and offers surprising discoveries about Abbott's originals.

Levere was drawn first to sites that were largely intact, but those sites often presented the greatest technical difficulties. A case in point is the series of six views that Abbott took with a handheld Linhoff camera from the roof of One Wall Street, fifty-five stories above street level. Moving around the roof, Abbott exposed one view of Broadway, three of Wall Street, and two of Broad Street. During the four hours he was allowed access to the roof, Levere rephotographed the Broadway view and one of the Wall Street views (pages 38–41). The precariousness of leaning over the parapet convinced him that Abbott had pointed her camera without seeing exactly what she was photographing. To reproduce her spontaneous performance, he used a heavy tripod weighted with sandbags. Although Abbott had photographed in May, Levere was denied access in spring, when peregrine falcons nest on the roof and have been known to attack intruders.

Levere's photographs of sites that have changed greatly sometimes yielded aesthetic or historical contrasts that rival those of Abbott's images. In *Custom House Statues and New York Produce Exchange*, for example, Abbott juxtaposed the two beaux-arts sculptures situated in front of the U.S. Custom House at Bowling Green with the Victorian New York Produce Exchange, contrasting two historical eras in one image. The architecturally significant Produce Exchange was replaced in 1959 by an undistinguished office building. Nonetheless, Levere's 1997 rephotograph offers an equally engaging juxtaposition, now of the curvilinear sculptures with the grid of a mid-twentieth-century curtain-wall facade (pages 24–25).

More often, architectural changes produced less harmonious but still striking results. In Abbott's *Henry Street*, two grand Cass Gilbert skyscrapers—the Woolworth and Municipal buildings—rise up behind Lower East Side tenements, symbols of the city's most and least powerful communities. In Levere's 1998 version, the rhythmic row of tenements is broken by demolished buildings and obscured by parked cars and a stop sign; Cass Gilbert's "twin towers" are sandwiched between high-rise apartments and the twin towers of the World Trade Center, which loom in the background (pages 54–55). This visual cacophony succeeds in conveying how much more dense and complex the cityscape has become since the 1930s.

Sometimes the changes have been less fortuitous, resulting in what Levere calls "ugly" photographs. In *MacDougal Alley*, Abbott contrasted the soaring art deco setbacks of One Fifth Avenue with the picturesque two-story houses of a Greenwich Village alley. A massive postwar apartment building, which now blocks all but the water tower of One Fifth Avenue, destroyed Abbott's composition, and parked cars and a security gate mar the charm of the alley. To ameliorate the aesthetic damage, Levere adopted Abbott's practice of posing a passerby in the foreground (pages 112–113).

Many of Abbott's subjects are simply gone, and Levere could not attempt them. In some instances, however, he was able to identify a fragment of a building or a fire hydrant that allowed him to determine Abbott's camera position. In *William Goldberg*, the sign-encrusted loft building at the corner of Broadway and East Ninth Street has been replaced by an undistinguished postwar apartment building. Levere established what he calls Abbott's "authorship" by aligning the sidewalk curb, the only element of her image that remains (pages 110–111). He enlivened his composition by including two pedestrians, one carrying a huge bag of party balloons. Serendipitously, a one-way sign mounted on a traffic light in Levere's photograph echoes the arrow-shaped sign directing customers "one flight up" in Abbott's version. Despite these embellishments, Levere's image painfully illustrates the legacy of the postwar building boom.

In some cases, Abbott's subject was intact but the place where she stood was inaccessible or gone. An example is *Vanderbilt Avenue*, which shows the canyonlike effect of office buildings next to Grand Central Station. Levere photographed the scene through the foliage of a tree with a FedEx truck blocking his view, but Chase Manhattan Bank security staff insisted that he leave before he could produce a publishable image. When he tried to rephotograph *Triborough*

far left: Vanderbilt Avenue, Looking South from East Forty-Seventh Street, 1935 **left:** Vanderbilt Avenue, 1998 **right:** Luchow's Restaurant, 110 East Fourteenth Street between Third and Fourth Avenues, 1938 **far right:** Luchow's Restaurant, 1993

Bridge, 125th Street Approach, he was forced from the site by a security guard's threat that a helicopter SWAT team was on its way.

Timing was a major factor in Levere's success or failure. He missed photographing Luchow's, a legendary restaurant near Union Square, which stood in ruins during a heated landmark battle in the early 1990s and was demolished in 1995 after a suspicious fire. After the destruction of the World Trade Center, many of Abbott's West Street sites were off limits for security reasons, but others, such as *Vista From West Street,* were newly revealed (pages 84–85). With permission from the Office of Emergency Management, Levere took this photograph before West Street was reopened to traffic and Abbott's camera position again became inaccessible.

In some cases, Levere attempted to rephotograph but rejected his results because they did not meet his exacting technical standards. In *Washington Square, Looking North,* Levere discovered that the tree framing the left side of Abbott's photograph had been carved into a totem pole, an eloquent reminder of Washington Square Park's youth culture. Despite his best efforts, he could not eliminate the "vignette" effect at the top edge of the image as successfully as Abbott had done. Another rejected image is *Lamport Export Company,* which shows a cast iron building on Broadway between Broome and Spring streets, around the corner from Levere's own apartment. Textile wholesalers used the building from 1872 to 1998, when the New York Sports Club and Old Navy moved in. The contrast between Abbott and Levere's photographs illustrates the emergence of SoHo as a fashionable neighborhood. But, as a close examination of the right edge of his image reveals, Levere could not perfectly duplicate the grid of Abbott's composition.

Like Abbott, Levere worked intuitively without an overall plan, focusing on each photograph as a separate experience and with a deep affection for an ever-changing city. The mood of Abbott's project, however, is markedly different from Levere's. Despite the difficulties of the Depression, Abbott's New York evokes the boundless optimism of the 1920s building boom. Her grand ambition—to document the archetypal modern city through the quintessentially modern medium of photography—was typical of her generation. Levere's New York, marred by decades of often indifferent architecture and shaken by the destruction of the World Trade Center, is decidedly less heroic. Like much of the best art of his generation, his photographs offer an unsettling critique of modern urban life. In paying homage to Abbott's project, Levere has given us a unique opportunity to evaluate ourselves.

far left: Washington Square, Looking North, 1936 **left:** Washington Square, Looking North, 1998 **right:** Lamport Export Company, 1935 **far right:** Lamport Export Company, 2002

PLATES

DOWNTOWN MANHATTAN, EAST

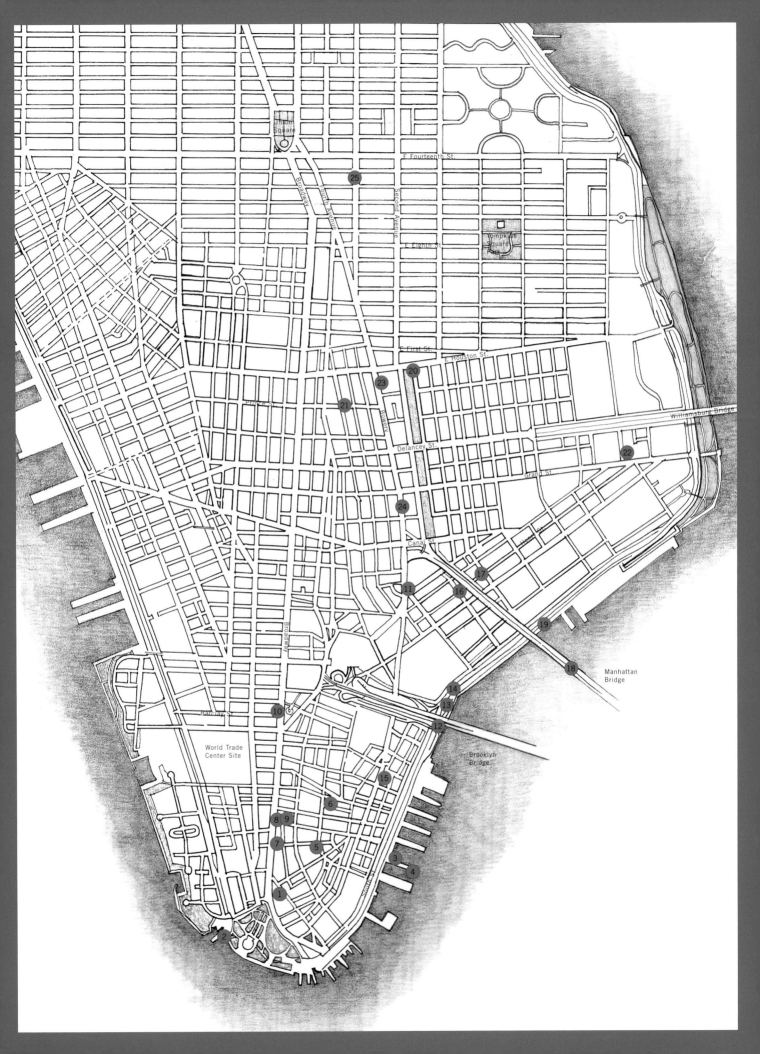

Custom House Statues and New York Produce Exchange, Bowling Green, 1936

When a new Custom House was built in 1907, the entrance was adorned with four allegorical sculptures representing the continents. Abbott photographed two of the statues, using the New York Produce Exchange (1886) as a backdrop to contrast the Victorian era with the Gilded Age. In 1959 the Produce Exchange replaced its nineteenth-century palazzo with a modernist office building, now the property of the Metropolitan Transit Authority. When Levere photographed the scene in 1997, the MTA building stood empty in preparation for a complete renovation.

Statues in front of Former Custom House and MTA Headquarters, 1997

Firehouse, Battery, 1936

At the tip of Manhattan is Castle Clinton, a fortress built for the War of 1812 that
in Abbott's time housed the city aquarium and was a major tourist attraction. It
was designated a national monument in 1950 and now serves as the ticket center
for ferries to Ellis Island and the Statue of Liberty. In her photograph, Abbott
focused on the Victorian firehouse that stood in front of the aquarium. With the
firehouse demolished and replaced by landfill, it was difficult for Levere to locate
Abbott's exact camera position.

Castle Clinton, Battery, 2002

Downtown Skyport, 1936
Foot of Wall Street

From Pier 11, Abbott photographed the city-owned skyport, built in 1934 to dock amphibious planes that shuttled Westchester County commuters to work on Wall Street. To take his photograph, Levere stood inside a new ferry slip terminal built in 2001 by New York Waterways. The girl standing at the railing in the foreground of his picture is reminiscent of the two shoeshine boys that Abbott included in her image.

Downtown Ferry Port, 2001

Manhattan I, 1936
From Pier 11, East River, between Old Slip and Wall Street

In her 1936 photograph, Abbott captured the major towers of Manhattan's downtown skyline. Six decades later, Levere found 1960s office buildings blocking
Abbott's panoramic view, although the apex of 60 Wall Street was still visible. Pier
11 was demolished in 1938, and Levere stood on a temporary pier that docked a
water shuttle to LaGuardia Airport. In 2001 a ferry slip was constructed on the site.

Manhattan I, 1998

Stone and William Streets, 1936

Abbott relished the challenge of photographing skyscrapers rising from the dark, winding streets of the financial district. Exchange Place, which Abbott mislabeled as Stone Street, was a particularly narrow alley in the heart of the district. The principal buildings seen in Abbott's photograph remain, but the pedestrian bridge spanning Exchange Place is gone, and the picturesque crook-handled lampposts have been replaced with modern gooseneck streetlights.

Exchange Place and William Street, 1997

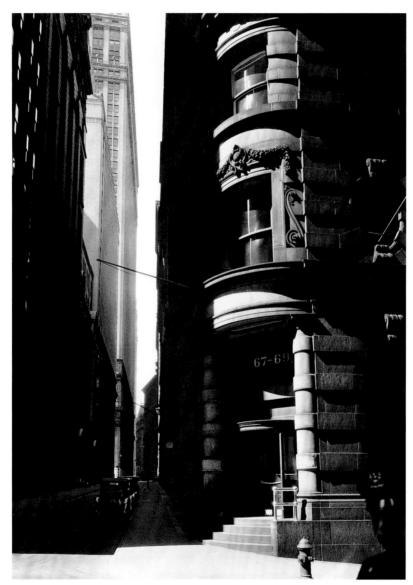

Cedar Street from William Street, 1936

Lined with skyscrapers, William Street was a dark place even on the bright day that Abbott photographed it. Only the facade of the Mutual Life Insurance Company of New York Building (1897) was touched by the sun. In 1960 the entire block was demolished to make way for Chase Manhattan Plaza, designed by Skidmore, Owings & Merrill, which brought the International Style to the financial district. The scaffolding seen in Levere's photograph was erected for the cleaning of Jean Dubuffet's bronze sculpture *Group of Four Trees* (1972) in the aftermath of September 11.

Cedar Street from William Street, 2002

Canyon: Broadway and Exchange Place, 1936

To achieve the vertiginous "canyon" effect in her image, Abbott stood on Exchange Place facing Broadway and pointed her camera upward. The Adams Building (61 Broadway, 1914) at the center of her photograph still stands, but the flanking buildings at 42 and 60 Broadway, with their heavy cornices, have been replaced by taller, sleeker towers.

Canyon: Broadway and Exchange Place, 1997

Broadway to the Battery, 1938
From the Roof of One Wall Street

From the roof of the Irving Trust Company (1930), Abbott took several photographs of the financial district, among them a bird's eye view of Broadway. Since Abbott's day, the Hudson River piers have been demolished, and Battery Park City has been developed into a neighborhood of its own. When Levere took his photograph in 1997, the octagonal Museum of Jewish Heritage (top right) had just opened at Battery Place.

Broadway to the Battery, 1997

overleaf

Wall Street District, 1938 and 1997

From the Roof of One Wall Street

Another bird's eye view taken from the Irving Trust Company roof is Abbott's
photograph of Wall Street between Broadway and the East River. The visual
of Abbott's image has been diminished by the addition of several new skyscrapers
that today crowd Wall Street, blocking the view of the East River and masking the
stepped tower of 120 Wall Street at water's edge.

Woolworth Building, 1936
233 Broadway

The Woolworth Building, the world's tallest building from 1913 to 1930, was the
first skyscraper to use the imagery of a Gothic cathedral. Abbott's foreshortened
and distorted image emphasizes the building's bulk and delicate detail. Levere was
unable to reproduce Abbott's fortuitous accident—the flared light that reflected
off her lens from the building's windows.

Woolworth Building, 2002

"El," Second and Third Avenue Lines, 250 Pearl Street, 1936

In Abbott's time, the El divided the waterfront to the east (left) from the financial district to the west (right). The El was demolished in 1955, and two full-block office buildings were erected on the east side of Pearl Street in the 1970s. With the El gone, the enormous 60 Wall Tower (1932, now 70 Pine Street) is more visible; just behind it is the even larger 60 Wall Street (1988).

250 Pearl Street, 2002

Brooklyn Bridge with Pier 21, Pennsylvania Railroad, 1937

Deliberately avoiding familiar views, Abbott photographed the Brooklyn Bridge from South Street at the entrance to the Pennsylvania Railroad pier shed, now demolished. With the F.D.R. Drive overhead, the bridge with its familiar cable construction is hardly visible in Levere's image. When he visited the site in 2002, the supports of the drive were being painted, and the area was cleared of the usual parked cars.

Brooklyn Bridge from under the F.D.R. Drive, 1998

Waterfront, South Street, 1935

Where James Slip, South Street, and Front Street converge, Abbott captured an
expansive view of the lower Manhattan skyline, with the spires of 60 Wall Tower
(1932) and 40 Wall Street (1929) rising above the entry ramp of the Brooklyn
Bridge. In Levere's photograph, the F.D.R. Drive entry ramp (left) and several
flat-topped skyscrapers complicate the view.

Waterfront, South Street, 2002

South Street and James Slip, 1937

Fifteen months after photographing *Waterfront, South Street*, Abbott returned to
the site. Standing slightly to the south and using a wider lens, she focused on the
old commercial buildings of the waterfront rather than the skyline. In 1952 the
Governor Alfred E. Smith Houses replaced those buildings, removing the remnants
of maritime commerce. Levere stood under the F.D.R. Drive to photograph the scene.

South Street and James Slip, 2002

overleaf
"El," Second and Third Avenue Lines, Bowery and Division Street, 1936
Bowery and Division Street, 2002

In Abbott's day, two subway lines converged at Chatham Square, creating an
unusually large web of train tracks overhead. The elevated trains were demolished
in 1942 (Second Avenue) and 1955 (Third Avenue), and in 1961 the massive
Chatham Green apartments replaced the neighborhood's tenements. The corner
window of one remaining building (far right) allowed Levere to establish Abbott's
camera position in an otherwise completely transformed site.

Henry Street, 1935
Henry and Market Streets, Looking West

Abbott's photograph contrasts some of the city's oldest tenements with the grand spires of the pre–World War I Woolworth (1913) and Municipal (1915) buildings. While the early skyscrapers and tenements remain, the view has become more complex, with increased traffic crowding the foreground and the Southbridge Towers (1969) rising in the middle distance. When Levere photographed the scene in 1998, the twin towers of the World Trade Center dwarfed everything around them.

Henry Street, 1998

Pike and Henry Streets, 1936
Pike between Henry and Madison Streets

Looking east on Henry Street, Abbott used a long lens to create the illusion that
these Lower East Side tenements loomed up to the Manhattan Bridge, six blocks
away. With the construction of the Rutgers Houses (1964) and the widening of
Henry Street, the tunnel-like effect of Abbott's photograph could not be duplicated.
When Levere photographed the scene, Con Edison had blocked off the street, which
is normally filled with three lanes of fast-moving traffic.

Pike and Henry Streets, 1997

Manhattan Bridge, Looking Up, 1936

Standing on the southern pedestrian walkway and looking straight up, Abbott transformed a supporting pier of the Manhattan Bridge (1909) into an "Eiffel Tower." In 2001, when the bridge reopened after a three-year renovation, a new walkway fence partially obstructed Levere's view. As a result, the lower portion of his photograph is slightly out of focus.

Manhattan Bridge, Looking Up, 2001

Oyster Houses, South Street and Pike Slip, 1937

For more than a century, merchants sold Long Island oysters from houseboats docked along the East River. In 1937, when Abbott photographed the last of these oyster houses, other merchants had moved inland to the Fulton Fish Market. In 2002 this stretch of the waterfront under the F.D.R. Drive had just been renovated for recreational use.

South Street and Pike Slip, 2002

Old Law Tenements, 1937
35–47 1/2 East First Street

In 1930 a row of Houston Street buildings was torn down, revealing the backs of
these East First Street tenements. Abbott photographed the site in 1937, when a
WPA playground was under construction on Houston Street. Today the tenements
are intact, while the playground is now used as storage for an architectural salvage
company. Abbott incorporated a lamppost and mailbox in her composition to lend
visual interest to the foreground; Levere created a similar effect by including a taxi
in his photograph.

Old Law Tenements, 2002

Mulberry and Prince Streets, 1935

Shortly after Abbott photographed this Federal house "for sale or for lease," it and
the adjacent building were torn down. The surrounding structures have remained,
and the site is currently a parking lot. What was the heart of Little Italy in 1935 is
now NoLIta, "north of Little Italy," where chic boutiques and upscale restaurants
are replacing Italian bakeries and social clubs. In Levere's photograph, the pent-
house under construction on the roof of a tenement building (right) testifies to the
neighborhood's transformation.

Mulberry and Prince Streets, 1998

Grand Street, Nos. 511–513, 1937
Between Sheriff and Columbia Streets

These early nineteenth-century houses were built when Grand Street was a
major commercial thoroughfare connecting the East River to the Bowery. Abbott
chose to photograph these mundane structures instead of the Amalgamated
Dwellings (1930), a famous experiment in modernist workers' housing, which
stood across the street. Today the neighborhood is dominated by new low- and
middle-income housing complexes.

Grand Street, Nos. 511–513, 2002

Tri-boro Barber School, 264 Bowery, 1935

During the Depression, the Bowery was filled with barber schools whose students were primarily flophouse lodgers seeking a path out of poverty. When Levere photographed the storefront, a typical Bowery restaurant supply shop had recently been replaced by Sosinna's Café.

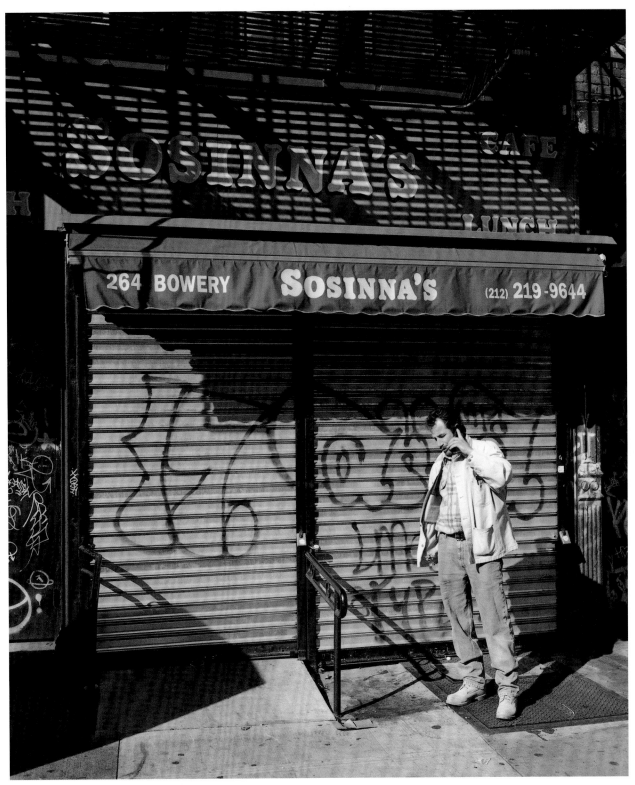

Sosinna's Café, 264 Bowery, 2002

Blossom Restaurant, 103 Bowery, 1935

In the 1930s, the Bowery was a well-established refuge for the homeless, lined with flophouses offering rooms at thirty cents a night and meals for as little as fifteen cents. The Boston Hotel, with its first floor occupied by the Blossom Restaurant, was such an establishment. Today the Bowery, lodged between the East Village and Chinatown, is rapidly gentrifying. The current occupant of 103 Bowery sells housewares to a predominantly Asian clientele.

Everyware Co., Inc., 103 Bowery, 1998

Lyric Theatre, 1936
100 Third Avenue between Twelfth and Thirteenth Streets

Built in 1880, the Lyric Theatre was converted to a movie house in 1910.
Located only a few blocks from the Bowery, its Depression-era clientele consisted
mostly of transients, who for ten cents could see a newsreel, a short subject,
and two features. The intricate detailing of the old theater has been removed, but
the building is still a theater today, showing gay adult films.

CVC Cinemas, 2001

DOWNTOWN MANHATTAN, WEST

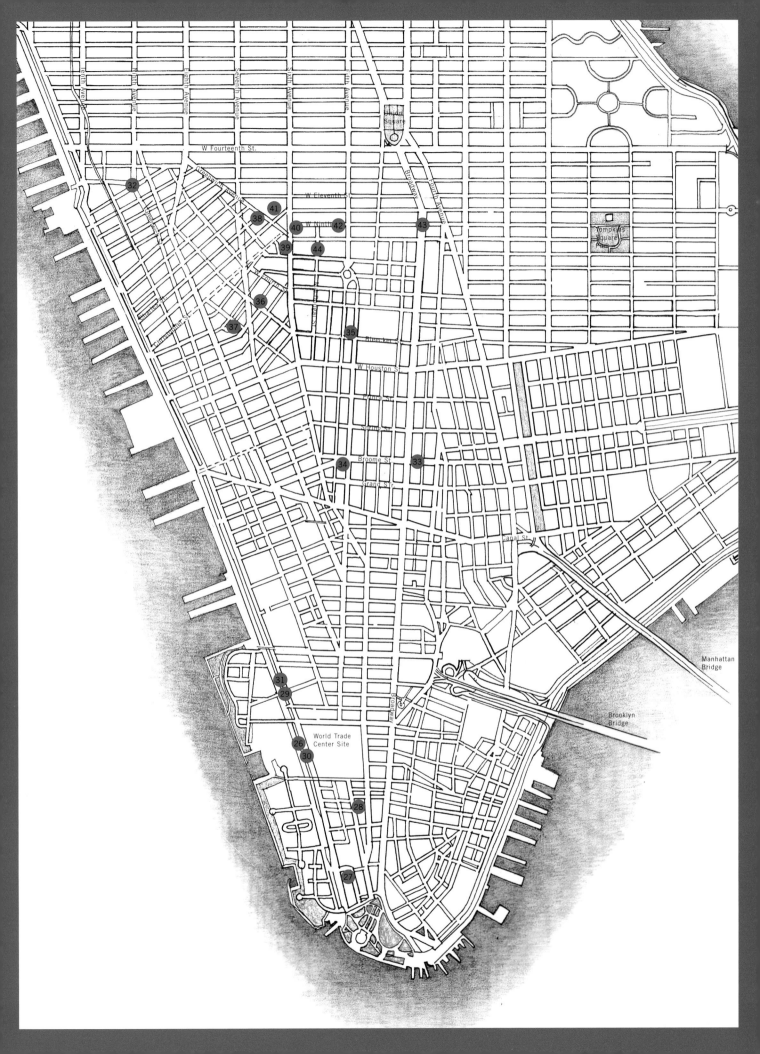

New York Telephone Building, 1936
140 West Street

When the award-winning New York Telephone Building, designed by Ralph Walker of Voorhees, Gmelin and Walker, was constructed in 1926, it rose behemoth-like above acres of shabby waterfront buildings. Its dominance over the area ended in the 1970s with the construction of the World Trade Center, its neighbor to the south. In Levere's photograph, the scaffolding and tarpaulins at the top of the building's tower are evidence of damage, still not repaired, from the Trade Center's collapse.

Verizon Communications Building, 2002

overleaf
Construction Old and New
38 Greenwich Street from 37 Washington Street, 1936
Above the Brooklyn Battery Tunnel, 2002

Abbott took advantage of an empty lot to contrast the nineteenth-century
tenements near the Hudson River waterfront with Broadway's new office towers.
In 1946 the tenements, along with this stretch of Greenwich and Washington
streets, were demolished to build the Brooklyn Battery Tunnel, which opened in
1950. Levere's photograph shows a pedestrian bridge that crosses the roadway
at the tunnel entrance.

Vista, Thames Street, 1938
22 Thames Street between Greenwich Street and Trinity Place

Thames Street is a one-block alley at the edge of the financial district. As in
Construction Old and New, Abbott sought to contrast the nineteenth-century
remnants of the waterfront with the recently erected soaring skyscrapers.
Today, high-rises built for New York University's Graduate School of Business
Administration occupy both sides of Thames Street, leaving only a sliver of
Abbott's vista.

Vista, Thames Street, 1999

West Street between Murray and Warren Streets, 1936

This West Street view shows the New York Telephone Building in context. In the 1960s the small commercial buildings were torn down as part of the Washington Market Urban Renewal Project. In 1983 several insurance companies funded the College of Insurance, which occupies the center of Levere's photograph.

West Street between Murray and Warren Streets, 2001

Vista from West Street, Nos. 115–118 between Dey and Cortlandt Streets, 1938

Abbott moved farther south for this view of West Street's old buildings and the towers of the financial district. The block was demolished in the 1970s for the construction of the World Trade Center, which completely obstructed the view of the distant office buildings. After September 11, Abbott's vista was restored but access to the site was restricted until the spring of 2002, when Levere was allowed to work at the perimeter of Ground Zero.

Vista from West Street, Former World Trade Center Site, 2002

West Street, Row I, Nos. 178–182, 1936

In Abbott's photograph *West Street, Row I,* the waterfront's proximity to the financial district is barely discernible. Only after these buildings were demolished in the 1960s did the spire of the nearby Woolworth Building become visible from the site. Levere's photograph shows the one remaining building, whose tenant won a court battle to prevent the city from demolishing his home until new construction plans were finalized. Although the "hold-out" structure was torn down in 2003, the new building's plans are still in dispute.

West Street, No. 179, 2001

Gansevoort Street, No. 53, 1936

A triangular lot prompted the odd shape of this commercial loft building near the Gansevoort Market on the periphery of Greenwich Village. Photographed from the side, it looks like a stage set. Ironically, when Levere visited the site, a movie was being shot there. The neighborhood, recently designated the Gansevoort Market Historic District, has become ultra-chic.

Gansevoort Street, No. 53, 2002

Broadway near Broome Street, 1935

The 1895 Italianate skyscraper on Broadway and the warehouses on Broome Street lie within SoHo's cast-iron landmark district and remain architecturally unchanged. The wholesalers of Abbott's era, however, have been replaced by fashionable retailers and residents.

Broadway near Broome Street, 1998

Broome Street, Nos. 512–514, 1935
Between Thompson Street and West Broadway

In Abbott's photograph, two once-elegant federal houses are seen against an
industrial warehouse as trucks head for the Holland Tunnel entrance two blocks
west. Soon after Abbott photographed the site, the old houses were replaced
with small commercial buildings. The warehouse remains but, like many others
in this area, has been renovated into luxury SoHo apartments.

Broome Street, Nos. 512–514, 1998

Mori Restaurant, 1935
144 Bleecker Street

Founded in 1884, Mori's was a popular restaurant serving traditional Italian food to New Yorkers and tourists for more than fifty years. The restaurant's unusual facade, which combined 144 and 146 Bleecker Street, was designed by modernist architect Raymond Hood, who lived nearby. Today, Hood's design is barely visible, and the two entrances—to a video store and nightclub—have been restored.

Kim's Video and the Elbow Room, 2001

overleaf
Bread Store, 1937 and 1998
259 Bleecker Street

In 1920 Anthony Zito opened an Italian bakery on the ground floor of a Bleecker Street tenement. For many years a copy of Abbott's 1937 photograph hung behind the counter of this family-run business, which closed in 2004. When Levere photographed the shop, a salesperson artfully arranged the window display and posed for him. The movement of the sun allowed Levere only five minutes to capture the reflections of the buildings across the street in the Zito's shop window.

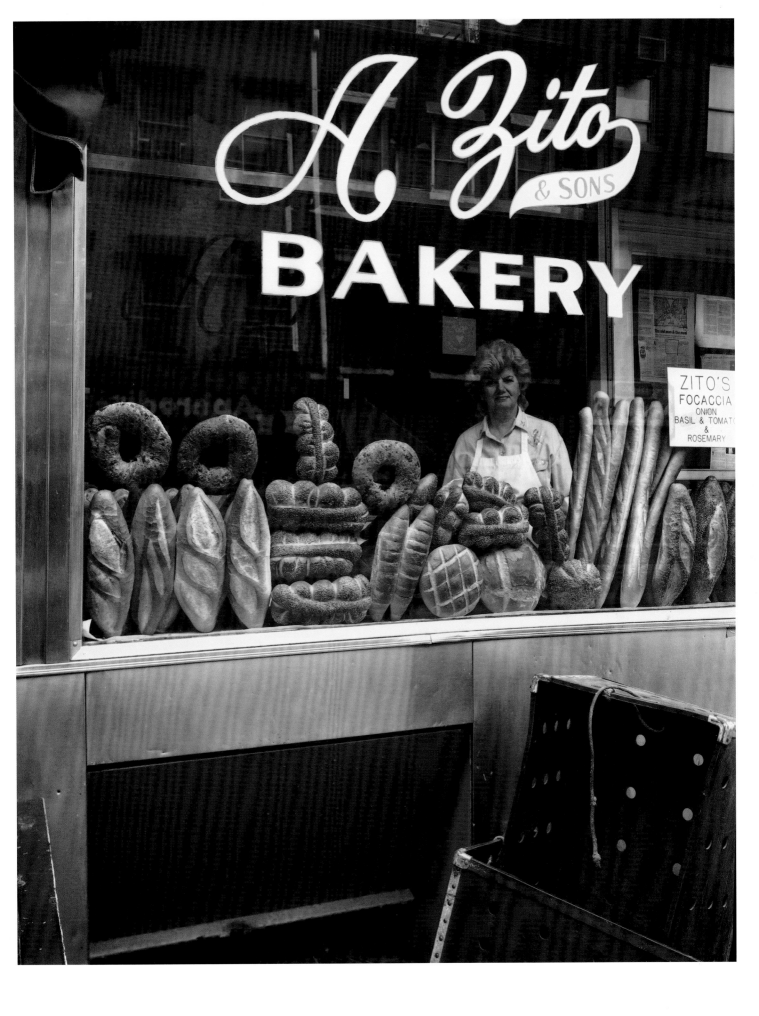

Commerce Street, Nos. 39–41, 1937

These twin houses stood across the street from Abbott's own Greenwich Village loft. Relatively unchanged, they show subtle signs of renovation, such as the oddly decorated window lintels. While the empty street in Abbott's view suggests a timeless serenity, Levere's photograph is cluttered with signs of modern life, including an illegally parked car.

Commerce Street, Nos. 39–41, 2001

Doorway, 16–18 Charles Street, 1938
Between Greenwich Avenue and Waverly Place

This highly eccentric doorway was the result of a renovation that combined two
pre–Civil War houses, incorporating an original doorway and two oval windows
at basement level. Today the house is painted pink, rendering it even more uncon-
ventional than in Abbott's time.

Doorway, 16–18 Charles Street, 2002

Gay Street, Nos. 14–16, 1937
Between Christopher Street and Waverly Place

In the early nineteenth century, many African Americans lived on Gay Street, which was named for abolitionist Sidney Howard Gay. By Abbott's day, the street had become a famous bohemian haunt. Number 14 was home to Ruth McKenney, who made the address famous in her book *My Sister Eileen*, a collection of stories about aspiring artists living cheaply in Greenwich Village garrets. The 1938 publication inspired the 1953 musical *Wonderful Town*. In 2003 David Ryan, the long-time tenant who lived in the basement apartment once shared by the McKenney sisters, was tragically killed in a fire there.

Gay Street, Nos. 14–16, 1997

overleaf
Jefferson Market Court, 1935
Jefferson Market Library, 2000

The Jefferson Market Court, built in 1877 on the site of an open market, remains one of Greenwich Village's most notable landmarks. When Abbott took her photograph, the Sixth Avenue El still ran in front of it. In the 1960s, the Ruskinian Gothic courthouse, designed by Calvert Vaux and Frederick C. Withers, became a cause célèbre for preservationists, and in 1967 it was renovated as a branch of the New York Public Library. In Abbott's photograph, the tower clock reads 10:30, but in Levere's image the time is 11:30 due to daylight savings time.

Patchin Place with Jefferson Market Court in Background, 1937
Off West Tenth Street between Sixth and Greenwich Avenues

These ten small houses were built in a cul-de-sac behind the Jefferson Market
Library in 1848 for workers at the nearby Brevoort Hotel. In Abbott's day, several
artists and writers lived there, including her close friend Djuna Barnes (1892–
1982). The buildings were saved from demolition in 1963 and granted landmark
status in 1969.

Patchin Place with Jefferson Market Library in Background, 1997

Brevoort Hotel with Mark Twain House, 1935
Fifth Avenue between East Eighth and Ninth Streets

The Brevoort Hotel (1851) was one of New York's oldest, and its café was a favorite hangout for Village artists and writers. Between 1904 and 1908, Mark Twain, then at the height of his fame, lived in the house next door, which was designed by architect James Renwick in 1840. In 1954 the entire block was razed for the nineteen-story Brevoort Apartments.

Brevoort Apartments, 1999

William Goldberg, 1937
771 Broadway at East Ninth Street

Standing in front of the famous Wanamaker's department store (razed by fire in
1956) and passing up neighborhood landmarks like Grace Church and Cooper
Union, Abbott photographed this commercial loft covered with advertisements.
In 1953 it was replaced by a fifteen-story apartment building.

Broadway and Ninth Street, 2002

MacDougal Alley, 1936
From MacDougal Street between West Eighth Street and Washington Square North

MacDougal Alley originally housed stables that by Abbott's day had been converted
to residences favored by artists and writers. The contrast of the quaint nineteenth-
century buildings with One Fifth Avenue (1929) soaring up at the end of the alley
was an irresistible picture postcard view. In 1955 the construction of the mammoth
Two Fifth Avenue ruined the vista by blocking the art deco landmark.

MacDougal Alley, 2002

MIDTOWN

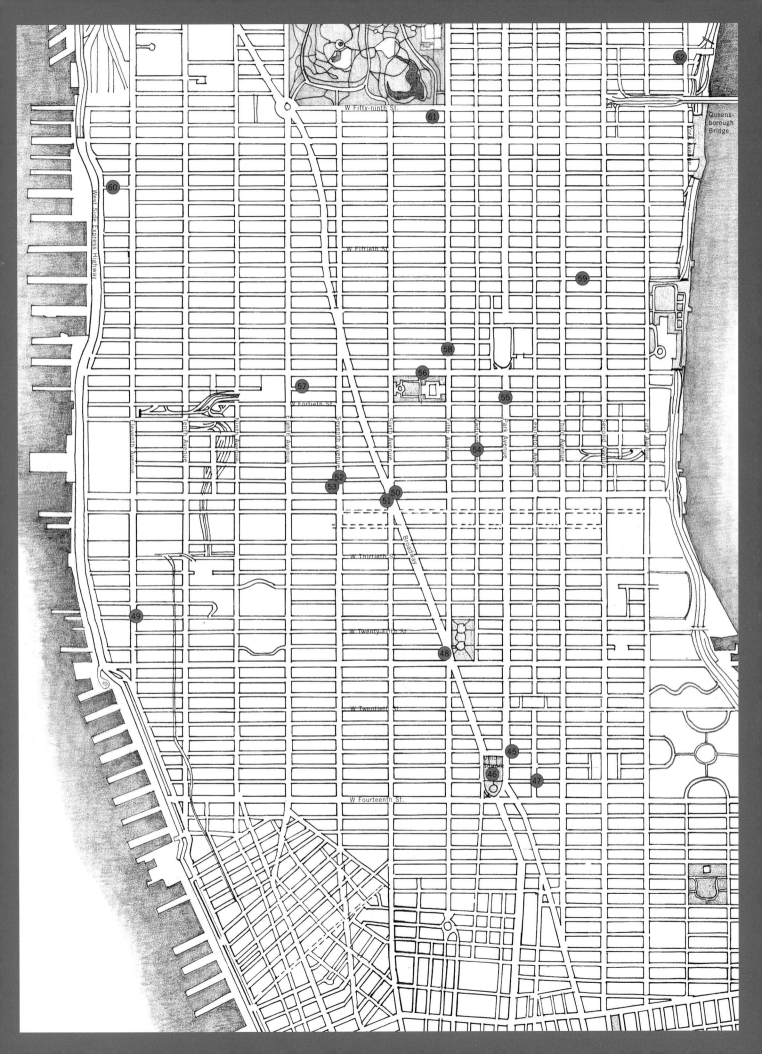

Union Square West, Nos. 31–41, 1938

At the northeast corner of Union Square, Abbott photographed an entire block of
nineteenth-century commercial buildings. Except for no. 39, which was replaced
by a one-story McDonald's, the block remains intact. The strong diagonal shadow
that unifies Abbott's composition is missing in Levere's photograph, due to a new
building behind no. 31.

Union Square West, Nos. 31–41, 1999

Union Square, 1936
Fourth Avenue between East Fifteenth and Sixteenth Streets

In the 1920s, Union Square became a working-class shopping mecca whose main
attraction was the S. Klein department store on Broadway. Abbott juxtaposed
the popular store with the bronze statue of Lafayette, which was given to New York
by France to commemorate the centennial of the American Revolution. Today,
Toys 'R' Us has replaced S. Klein, and the former Union Savings bank is an off-
Broadway theater. The Zeckendorf Towers, built in 1987 (right), obstruct the
view of the Con Edison tower, while the sapling in Abbott's photograph has become
a full-grown tree.

Union Square, 2002

Irving Place Theatre, 1938
118–120 East Fifteenth Street

Built in the 1880s, when the city's theater district was centered in Union
Square, the Irving Place Theatre became a burlesque house in the early 1930s,
where stripper Gypsy Rose Lee launched her career. It was later used as a
warehouse for S. Klein and, in 1985, was demolished for the twenty-seven-story
Zeckendorf Towers.

Irving Place Theatre, 2002

Flatiron Building, 1938

Built at the intersection of Fifth Avenue and Broadway in 1902, the Flatiron
Building, nicknamed for its shape, became an instant symbol of modernity. Abbott
captured the building's symbolic status with her foreshortened, truncated view
that converted the building into an arrow in space. While Abbott hazarded busy
traffic to take her photograph, Levere was able to stand safely on a traffic island.
Today the Flatiron is the oldest remaining skyscraper in New York.

Flatiron Building, 2001

Starrett-Lehigh Building I, 1936
601 West Twenty-sixth Street between Eleventh and Twelfth Avenues

Designed by Cory & Cory and completed in 1931, the Starrett-Lehigh Building
was a famous modernist experiment in industrial architecture that allowed freight
cars to be moved along tracks from the Hudson River piers directly into the
building. It never functioned as intended, however, as trucking replaced shipping
and the waterfront declined. When nearby Chelsea was gentrified in the 1990s,
the building attracted many commercial clients, including Martha Stewart, who set
up her corporate headquarters there.

Starrett-Lehigh Building I, 2002

Herald Square, 1936

In 1902 R. H. Macy built "the world's largest department store," making Herald Square, where Broadway and Sixth Avenue cross at Thirty-fourth Street, the city's main shopping district. The Sixth Avenue El is visible in the foreground of Abbott's image, and a remnant of the original Herald Building stands in the triangular plot that today is a small green oasis in the midst of the two heavily trafficked avenues. The site remains largely unchanged, if less fashionable than it once was.

Herald Square, 2002

Herald Square, 1936

Abbott took a second photograph of Herald Square, focusing on the busy intersection of Thirty-fourth Street and Broadway. In a rare instance, she cropped her final print to focus more closely on the dense motor and pedestrian traffic around Macy's. Levere did not crop his version of the image, leaving his print full-frame.

Herald Square, 1997

overleaf

Seventh Avenue Looking North from Thirty-fifth Street, 1935 and 2001 (pp. 130–131)
Seventh Avenue Looking South from Thirty-fifth Street, 1935 and 2001 (pp. 132–133)
From the Nelson Tower at 450 Seventh Avenue

From an upper terrace of the forty-six-story Nelson Tower, Abbott photographed the canyon created by new skyscrapers in the heart of the garment district. Most of the buildings remain intact, with the important exceptions of the Metropolitan Opera (*Looking North*, top center), replaced by an office tower in 1969, and Pennsylvania Station (*Looking South*, lower right), demolished in 1965. For Levere, the timing of these photographs was particularly challenging, since the slow exposures his camera required were only possible when traffic was stopped at the light; with the sun moving quickly, Levere had only five minutes to take both photographs.

J. P. Morgan House, 1937
231 Madison Avenue at Thirty-sixth Street

This brownstone mansion was built in 1855, when Murray Hill was home to
many of New York's wealthiest families. In 1895 financier J. P. Morgan bought
and remodeled the house, which belonged to his son when Abbott photographed it. Today the building remains intact and houses offices for the Pierpont
Morgan Library.

J. P. Morgan House, 2002

Murray Hill Hotel: Spiral, 1935

Built in 1888, the Murray Hill Hotel was celebrated for its rich and powerful clientele. Known in the 1930s as the "Old Lady," it was famous as a reminder of New York's Victorian heyday. Abbott contrasted the hotel's spiraling cast-iron balconies with the geometric setbacks of a forty-five-story skyscraper at 22 East Fortieth Street. The hotel was replaced in 1947 with an office tower.

112 Park Avenue at East Fortieth Street, 2002

Fortieth Street between Sixth and Seventh Avenues, 1938
From the Salmon Tower at 11 West Forty-second Street

The Salmon Tower, facing Bryant Park, afforded Abbott with an unobstructed
southwest view of midtown office buildings. In Levere's photograph, the simplicity
of Abbott's composition is marred by three mundane structures that replaced the
six-story commercial buildings along Sixth Avenue and obscured the elegant facade
of the World Tower Building (1915, right).

Fortieth Street between Sixth and Seventh Avenues, 2002

McGraw-Hill Building, 1936
330 West Forty-second Street between Eighth and Ninth Avenues

When it opened in 1931, the McGraw-Hill Building, which housed the publishing firm's offices and printing presses, was scorned by traditionalists for its sleek functionalism and by orthodox modernists for its blue-green terracotta surface. Abbott contrasted the building with a quaint chalet-style station of the Ninth Avenue El. In Levere's photograph, Port Authority's massive bus ramps replace the El platform. With the decline of Times Square in the 1970s, McGraw-Hill moved to offices on Sixth Avenue, but the building has landmark status and provides office space to a variety of businesses.

McGraw-Hill Building, 2002

Tempo of the City I, 1938
Fifth Avenue and Forty-fourth Street

Then as now, midtown Fifth Avenue was a major retail district, filled with office workers, tourists, and shoppers. Using a handheld camera, Abbott took her photograph from the top of a double-decker bus stalled in traffic. To duplicate Abbott's shot, Levere rented a double-decker bus, but he could not gain permission to stop in traffic at midday. Eager to help, the bus driver feigned an emergency, placing orange cones on the road and opening the bus hood to allow Levere to take his photograph at precisely 1:10 P.M.

Tempo of the City I, 1997

Glass-Brick and Brownstone Fronts, 1938
209–211 East Forty-eighth Street

In 1934 Swiss-born architect William Lescaze remodeled an 1860s townhouse in
the International Style, complete with white stucco, glass brick, horizontal windows,
and a roof garden. Abbott contrasted the modernist experiment with its conventional
brownstone neighbor. While the Lescaze house remains relatively unchanged, the
adjacent house has been remodeled and the contrast lost.

209–211 East Forty-eighth Street, 1999

West Side Express Highway and Piers 95–98, 1937
From 619 West Fifty-fourth Street

In the late 1930s, an elevated West Side Highway was built to facilitate through-
traffic along the Hudson River piers. From the roof of a building used by Warner
Brothers Pictures, Abbott photographed a stretch of the highway a month after it
opened. As harbor industry declined, the highway fell into disrepair and was
torn down in 1982. The once busy piers lie abandoned in Levere's photograph. The
building from which Abbott captured her view is still occupied by film and video
companies.

West Street and Piers 95–98, 1998

overleaf
Central Park Plaza, 1937 and 2001
Fifth Avenue and Fifty-ninth Street

At the southeast corner of Central Park is the Central Park Plaza, surrounded by
some of the city's most luxurious hotels. With her back to the Plaza Hotel, Abbott
photographed one of the four basins of the Pulitzer Memorial Fountain (1916) as
well as three Fifth Avenue hotels built in the 1920s: the Pierre, the Sherry
Netherland, and the Savoy-Plaza (from left to right). In 1964 the Savoy-Plaza was
demolished for the fifty-story General Motors headquarters (slightly visible in the
top right corner of Levere's photograph). The two other hotels earned landmark
protection in 1981 with the designation of the Upper East Side Historic District.

Gas Tank and Queensboro Bridge, 1935
East Sixty-second Street and York Avenue

In the working-class neighborhood of Yorkville, Abbott photographed one of a group of three gas tanks that each filled an entire city block. In the 1930s, gas was still the primary fuel source of the city, despite New York's electrification after 1900. Not until the 1960s were the tanks finally demolished and replaced with apartment buildings. Levere's only point of reference was the Queensboro Bridge, which stands one block north and is barely visible through the leaves of a tree.

East Sixty-second Street and York Avenue, 2002

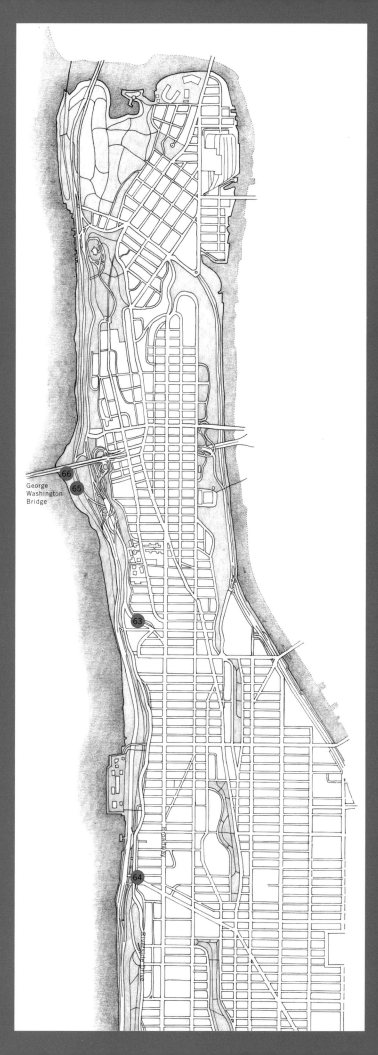

George
Washington
Bridge

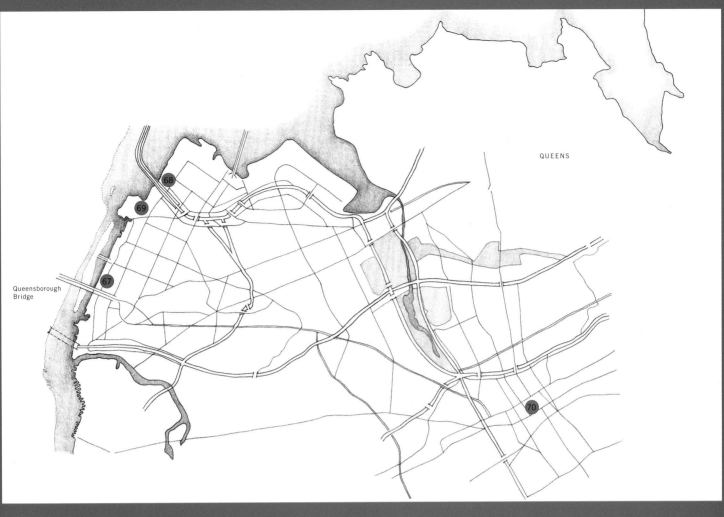

QUEENS

68
69
67
Queensborough
Bridge
70

81

STATEN ISLAND

Verrazano
Narrows
Bridge

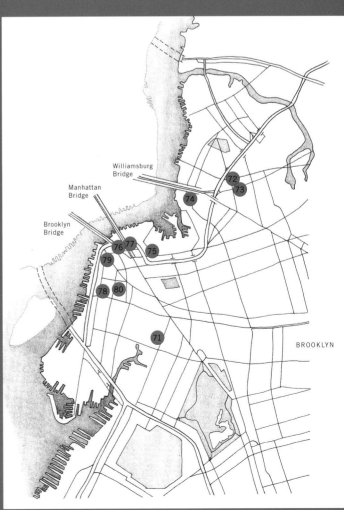

Williamsburg
Bridge
Manhattan
Bridge
Brooklyn
Bridge
72
73
74
76 77
75
79
78 80
71

BROOKLYN

Riverside Drive, No. 857, 1937
Between 158th and 159th Streets

Built in the 1890s, this modest clapboard house was surrounded by row houses
and an apartment building. The house remains, but its rural appearance has
diminished due to the loss of its porch and monitor roof and the addition of
"stone" siding.

Riverside Drive, No. 857, 1998

Under Riverside Drive Viaduct, 1937
West 125th Street and Twelfth Avenue

Built in 1901, the Riverside Drive Viaduct, which extends from 125th to 135th
streets, was an early attempt to relieve traffic congestion. Abbott photographed a
stretch of the viaduct near a massive gas tank at 131st Street, which was torn
down in 1961 for Manhattanville Houses, a public housing project. The viaduct
was rebuilt, after decades of neglect, in 1987.

Under Riverside Drive Viaduct, 2002

George Washington Bridge II, 1937

At the time of its completion in 1931, the George Washington Bridge was the longest suspension bridge in the world, almost twice the length of the Brooklyn Bridge. When Abbott photographed the bridge in 1937, the Henry Hudson Parkway was under construction. Levere stood deep in the woods on the far side of the parkway to rephotograph Abbott's shot.

George Washington Bridge II, 1998

George Washington Bridge I, 1936

To take her photograph of the bridge's east tower, Abbott stood in Fort Washington Park. Due to heightened security after September 11, Levere had to request permission from the Port Authority to gain access to the site. His photograph shows the bridge's lower roadway, added in 1962.

George Washington Bridge I, 2002

Queensboro Bridge II, 1937
From Long Island City, Queens

The Queensboro Bridge, which opened in 1909, spans Roosevelt Island (called
Welfare Island in the 1930s) to connect midtown Manhattan with Queens. Although
the East River side of New York harbor was in decline, the barge and tugboat in
Abbott's photograph demonstrates that it was still commercially active. The Welfare
Hospital of Chronic Diseases, demolished in 1994, was under construction in
1937, and its steel frame (left) is visible in front of the Manhattan skyline. Levere's
photograph shows Queensbridge Park running along the shoreline and a much
denser skyline, in which the spires of the Empire State Building and the Chrysler
Building are no longer dominant.

Queensboro Bridge II, 1997

Hell Gate Bridge I, 1937
From Astoria, Queens

Built in 1917 by the Penn Central Railroad, the Hell Gate Bridge is a vital link in
rail service between Canada and the South and West. Abbott photographed it from
Astoria Park, with a view of the Triborough Bridge in the distance.

Hell Gate Bridge I, 2002

Twenty-seventh Avenue, No. 1422, 1938
Astoria, Queens

The parish house of St. George's Episcopal Church, built in 1856, is still used by
the church today. A renovation has obscured the building's distinctive detailing.

Twenty-seventh Avenue, No. 1422, 2000

Jamaica Town Hall, 1937
Parsons Boulevard and Jamaica Avenue, Queens

After the 1898 consolidation of New York's five boroughs, the Queens town hall
became a courthouse. In 1941 the eclectic Victorian structure, which combined a
rusticated base, classical porch, and mansard roof, was torn down, and a large
McDonald's was built on the site in the 1980s.

McDonald's, 2002

Fourth Avenue, No. 154, 1936
Between Butler and Douglass Streets, Fort Greene, Brooklyn

These old-law tenements were built in the 1880s for Irish immigrants. During
the Depression, the landlord boarded them up rather than comply with new fire and
safety regulations. Among the many bills posted on the walls of the abandoned
buildings were posters for movies (*My Man Godfrey*) and a Democratic Party
campaign poster for President Franklin D. Roosevelt and Governor Herbert
K. Lehman. Surprisingly, the tenements survived and, with the revival of the Fort
Greene neighborhood, have been renovated.

Fourth Avenue, No. 154, 1998

Graham and Metropolitan Avenues, 1937
Williamsburg, Brooklyn

The opening of the Williamsburg Bridge in 1903 transformed the small village
of Williamsburg into a congested residential neighborhood. Despite development
in the surrounding area, these 1880s buildings in northern Williamsburg have
remained, shorn of their cornices, lintels, and roofline ornaments.

Graham and Metropolitan Avenues, 2002

Powers and Olive Streets, 1937
Williamsburg, Brooklyn

The Church of St. Nicholas, built in 1866 at the intersection of Powers and Olive
Streets, formed the heart of a German immigrant community in Williamsburg.
Although its belfry is now missing, the church building continues to function, as it
did in Abbott's day, as a Catholic school.

Powers and Olive Streets, 2002

overleaf
Williamsburg Bridge, 1937 and 2002
South Sixth and Berry Streets, Williamsburg

Opened in 1903, the Williamsburg Bridge was the second bridge to span the East River and greatly stimulated the development of Brooklyn's working-class neighborhoods. Abbott's photograph dramatically demonstrates how the bridge's entry ramp slashed through the waterfront community. Today the area's residents include many artists fleeing Manhattan's high rents.

Talman Street, Nos. 57–61, Brooklyn, 1936

In the shadow of the anchorage of the Manhattan Bridge was "Irishtown," a slum of pre–Civil War houses, many of which lacked cellars, heating, and plumbing. During the Depression, many African Americans took up residence there. Talman Street was cleared in 1950 to make way for the Brooklyn-Queens Expressway, whose entry ramps cut through the area. The neighborhood remained marginalized until the 1990s, when it became gentrified as DUMBO, "Down Under the Manhattan Bridge Overpass." The survival of the ice cream factory, seen in Abbott's photograph (upper right), allowed Levere to identify the site.

Park Triangle, Brooklyn, 2002
Between Jay, York, Talman, and Prospect Streets

Warehouse, Water and Dock Streets, Brooklyn, 1936

These warehouses on the waterfront beneath the Brooklyn Bridge, known as the
Empire Stores, were built in the 1870s, when the East River was the center of
New York's maritime industry. In the 1930s, they were used by the Yuban Coffee
Company to store coffee beans imported from South America. Empty for decades
after the company moved out in 1939, the warehouses were placed on the National
Register of Historic Places in 1974 and now stand in Empire Fulton Ferry State
Park, awaiting further renovation.

Warehouse, Water and Dock Streets, Brooklyn, 2002

overleaf

Brooklyn Bridge, Water and New Dock Streets, Brooklyn, 1936 and 2002

After photographing the Yuban Coffee warehouse, Abbott turned toward Manhattan to capture a view of the financial district skyline with the Brooklyn Bridge looming overhead. In Levere's version, a larger portion of the bridge is visible because the top three stories of the warehouse have been torn down. The building under construction in the middle distance of Abbott's photograph is a storage facility for the city's Purchasing Department; it will soon be demolished as part of the creation of the new Brooklyn Bridge Park.

Willow Place, Nos. 43–49, Brooklyn, 1936
Between Joralemon and State Streets

During the Depression, these four 1840s townhouses connected by a Greek
Revival colonnade were dilapidated and lacked central heating. They have now
been restored and stand within the Brooklyn Heights Historic District.

Willow Place, Nos. 43–49, Brooklyn, 2001

Willow Street, Nos. 131–137, Brooklyn, 1936

This is one of eight photographs of pre–Civil War houses in Brooklyn Heights that
Abbott took on a single day. In 1956 the wood-frame houses were demolished
for an apartment building. Levere's only points of reference were the stoop and tree
at the right edge of the composition.

Willow Street, No. 135, Brooklyn, 2001

Joralemon Street, No. 135, Brooklyn, 1936
Opposite Sidney Place between Clinton and Henry Streets

This Federal house was originally part of the Remsen farm, which encompassed much of Brooklyn Heights in the eighteenth and early nineteenth centuries. By the 1920s, however, an apartment building and an 1850s Victorian home flanked the house. Now within the Brooklyn Heights Historic District, it is intact but time-worn.

Joralemon Street, No. 135, Brooklyn, 2001

Garibaldi Memorial, 1937
Tompkins and Chestnut Avenues, Staten Island

From 1850 to 1854, famed Italian revolutionary Giuseppe Garibaldi took refuge
in the Staten Island cottage of his Florentine friend, the inventor Antonio Meucci.
In the 1880s, the Garibaldi Society acquired the house and in 1907, at the
centenary of Garibaldi's birth, constructed a concrete memorial to "protect as
well as glorify the poor, ungarnished wooden shrine." By 1952 the memorial had
so badly deteriorated that it was torn down, but the house is still maintained as
the Garibaldi-Meucci Memorial Museum.

Garibaldi Memorial, 1998

TECHNICAL NOTES

Cameras and lenses
Primary camera: 8x10 Century Universal with the following lenses:

- 7-inch F5.6 Goerz Dagor, Bausch & Lomb Compound shutter
- 9 1/2-inch F6.8 Goerz Dagor, Ilex Acme Synchro shutter
- 10 3/4-inch F6.8 Goerz Dagor, Alphax Synchromatic shutter
- 12-inch F6.8 Goerz Dagor, Ilex Acme Synchro shutter
- 14-inch F7.7 Goerz Dagor, Alphax Synchromatic shutter (Burke & James remount)

Linhof 4x5 Field Camera
Lens Schneider 90mm F5.6 Super-Angulon
Rolleiflex Series E, 75mm F3.5 Plannar

Using the same equipment as Abbott gave me certain advantages. Most importantly, the Dagor lenses she used have a large image circle, providing generous room for camera movements on the ground glass. As a result, Abbott was able to correct perspective distortions in many of her images. The lenses were made with very hard coatings and have survived well over the years. Remarkably, every Dagor lens I have encountered has been unscratched, although some are almost a hundred years old.

Processing
Developing the negatives proved difficult. Abbott's technique was to tray-process the film, which requires putting one's hands in the developing bath and working in complete darkness. As I did not like immersing my hands in the chemicals, I tried a series of commercial labs, all of which failed. One lab processed in trays, leaving big scratches on the negatives that occurred when the sharp corners of one negative hit another. A lab using deep developing tanks produced film with overdeveloped edges. A lab with a roller-transport system left the negatives covered with water spots. Finally I decided to process the film myself. The system that saved me was a Jobo rotary processor, which consisted of a drum with five holes for five sheets of 8x10 film. It was very simple to use and turned out beautiful negatives every time.

Printing
As the project came to a close, I bought an 8x10 Saltzman enlarger to print my images. Built in the World War II era, these enlargers, weighing nearly a half-ton, are sturdy and reliable. Nevertheless, I was dissatisfied with the test prints, which lacked some detail. After much experimenting and soul-searching, I decided to contact-print the negatives, as Abbott had done. I resisted the temptation to use a computer to alter or produce final prints. Like Abbott, I made traditional gelatin silver prints.

Reproducing Abbott's work
Reproducing Abbott's prints for this volume was another challenge. Abbott's signed and mounted vintage *Changing New York* prints at the Museum of the City of New York were made on a paper with a pebbled surface. This texture overwhelmed my attempt at straight photographic reproduction. I decided to polarize the light sources and lens, thus revealing virtually textureless images. The unavoidable compromise was a slight increase in the blacks.

DOUGLAS LEVERE is a New York-based photographer focused on newsmakers, celebrities, and architecture, working for advertising, corporate, and editorial clients. His images have appeared in *Newsweek*, *People*, *Business Week*, *Life*, *New York Times*, *Forbes*, and *Fortune*, among others.

BONNIE YOCHELSON is an art historian and former curator of prints and photographs at the Museum of the City of New York. She has written extensively on New York photography, including *Berenice Abbott: Changing New York, The Complete WPA Project* (The New Press and Museum of the City of New York, 1997).